GW01271776

God Became Man

To Include:

God's Almighty Power
God Is Light
God's Creative Power
God Speaks To Man

Neville Goddard

Contents

God Became Man   5

God's Almighty Power   11

God Is Light   20

God's Creative Power   29

God Speaks To Man   38

Contents

God Became Man

You are told that God became man that man may become God. You may think you are the man that God, as another, became, but I tell you: you are the God who became man, that man may become you! Because my visions which parallel scripture are accurate, I can boldly say that what I have just told you is true. In the 82nd Psalm we are the speaker, speaking to ourselves, saying: "I say, 'You are gods, sons of the Most High, all of you; nevertheless, you will die like men and fall as one man, O princes.'" We are the sons of the Most High, and we and our creator are one. Although we are now in a world of men, we have been promised that posterity will serve us and tell of the Lord who wrought it. You and I actually became human, that humanity may become spirit - as we are! You are not a little worm that God became. You were God before you devised the grand experiment, knowing it was the only way that man could become as you are!

Reverse your thinking: Think of yourself as God and you will have an entirely different feeling about becoming man. Although certain passages of scripture are not understood on this level, their meaning will be revealed, for we made everything because we loved it. Then we became man (man/woman) to raise and glorify our creations. We had to completely forget our true being in order to assume our creation and raise it to our level. The 22nd Psalm begins with our cry of despair: "My God, my God, why hast thou forsaken me?" but ends on this triumphant note: "Posterity will serve him; men will tell of the Lord to the coming generation and proclaim that he has wrought it to those that are yet unborn." This is not referring to another generation, but to the gods who have not yet discovered they came down, assumed human nature, and then accomplished what they set out to do.

The drama begins with the crucifixion, when God has union with man. It ends with the resurrection, when God raises man to the level of himself. Everyone will be raised to that level, because we are the gods who came down. The 82nd Psalm begins: "God has taken his place in the divine society; in the midst of the gods he holds judgment saying: 'Ye are gods, sons of the Most High, all of you; nevertheless, you will die like men and fall as one man, O princes.'" Dying in order to become man, we have assumed man's entire nature in order to raise man to the level of love, for in the end there is nothing but love. Look around and you will see what man has done, is doing, and is capable of doing and you will see the nature we took upon ourselves to raise it to the level of Infinite Love!

The crucifixion did not take place in the year 1 A.D., but in the beginning of time. The Bible begins, "In the beginning God." The word translated God is Elohim, which is a compound unity of one made of many. We are the gods who created the heavens and the earth. Many years ago, I relived that event by fulfilling the 42nd Psalm. Taken chronologically, this psalm appears to have happened in 1000 B.C., yet I remember when I became man. Hearing a voice in the depths of my soul proclaim I am God in the act of waking, I began to whirl in space and time. Then I felt myself being sucked into this crucifix. My hands were vortices, my feet vortices, my side a vortex and my head a vortex as I - life itself - became one with man. I was not man waiting for life; I was life which entered man. I took upon myself the cross that is man, to bear and raise it to the level of love. Everything - regardless of how horrible it seems to be - was made in love and must be raised to the level of love. One hundred and thirty-nine days after I awoke and rose from my tomb, God's only begotten son, David, revealed me as his father. I did not become the Father at that moment, I was always the Father, but came down and took upon myself the cross that is man, to raise him to the level of Fatherhood.

Now, in the 10th verse of the 22nd Psalm we read: "Deliver my life from the power of the dog." In the King James Version, the Hebrew word *yachid* is translated as "my darling", and as "my life" in the Revised Standard Version. The word first appears in the 22nd chapter, the 2nd and 16th verses of Genesis, where it is translated as "my only son". That is what the word *yachid* means in Hebrew. So, we see that the psalmist was asking to deliver his only son from the power of the dog. And in the 16th Psalm, David speaks, saying: "Thou wouldst not leave my soul in hell." Here the word translated "hell" means "uncovered; to disclose; to reveal; to take off the cover". In other words, do not leave me uncovered, but reveal me, that I - in turn - may reveal you; for the father will never be known save through his son, who must be uncovered.

The night I kept my promise, I exploded, and my son - he who had been concealed - was set free to reveal me as God the Father. I did not become God the Father, I was always he. I had purposely buried my son with me while I played the part of man. And then I unveiled my son so that he could reveal me as God the Father. The night I fulfilled the statement, deliver my only son from the power of the dog, I was possessed by a vision of two very handsome men standing at my side. They were about 40 years of age and were looking at my son - a lad about 12 or 13 - with lust beyond measure. Then I reminded them of David's victory over Goliath, as I pointed to his severed head on a table before me. Leaning against an open door, my son was looking out on a pastoral scene, while I was seated at his right - in fulfillment of the statement: "Thou art at my right, so I shall always be saved."

We are the gods who assumed human form. Now playing all the parts in the world, in time we will lift the part we are now playing up to our true self, who is God the Father. Before we descended, we were the Elohim who deliberately created the play; then we entered our creation to redeem it. Although this may seem arrogant, I know what I am talking about. Thomas Chancy, the editor of the *Encyclopedia Biblica* (which is one of the most scholarly of all the higher criticisms of the Bible) questioned how God could have taken his place in the divine assembly; yet I know that when we agreed to descend and dream in concert, the one made up of the many proclaimed: "I say, 'You are gods, sons of the Most High, all of you; nevertheless, you will die like men and fall as one man, O Princes.'" We are all princes, for we are the gods who made up the God who came down into mortal form, to raise these forms to the level of ourselves.

Man has completely reversed it. Today a prophetic book is all about mechanisms. More and better mechanics. Instead of plowing the field with a hoe, man now uses a tractor. Instead of a wheelbarrow, we use a missile to go to the moon. Man is making greater and greater mechanisms - but no one is telling of a Lordlier humanity! No one writes of that which came down into man and cannot return until he is born from above. No one is telling of this being who is going to rise out of his mortal skull and take man with him. Rather, they tell of greater and greater mechanisms.

Yet I tell you: the eternal story is that I - the I AM - took on mortality. I am the god who now wears your mortal form. The union is so complete, I feel I am human, and I will take this human feeling with me back into the level of love. We are the gods who came down in order to become individualized. What we will do tomorrow I do not know. Will we again descend into another element of the animal world? Or will it be the plant or mineral world we will redeem? We must redeem everything we have created, for we cannot leave anything unredeemed. So as Tennyson said in his poem called "The Plan": "Be patient. Our playwright will show in some fifth act what this wild drama means." I, the playwright of this wild drama, will not be satisfied just to redeem one section; the whole of creation must be redeemed. This has been quite a challenge, but God has wrought it as you are told in the end of this wonderful story. "Posterity will serve him and men will tell of the Lord to coming generations and proclaim that he has wrought it."

You are infinitely greater than you think you are. You and I were together in eternity, which is everlastingly enduring. What cannot endure forever ceases to be! When God ceases to imagine something, it vanishes. But you and I are eternal beings who came down into time. As Blake said, "We build mansions in eternity in these ruins of time."

Not one thing that has ever happened, is happening, or will happen, is out of kilter. It is all in order. Recently the Pope said that a man should not go against his conscience, but his conscience must be educated to conform to the doctrine of the church! Of all the nonsense in the world. Here is a man who sets himself up as the criterion of all that is right or wrong! Let us get back to scripture, for it hasn't a thing to do with this outside world of death!

Now, in the beginning we created the bull, the mule, the harlot, the homosexual, and the lesbian. We made everything because we loved it. So why, at the end of the drama, should two men look upon my only begotten son with such lust? To fulfill the 20th verse of the 22nd Psalm: "Deliver my only son from the power of the dog." - the power of the male temple harlot, for that is what the word "dog" means. Seeing the look of lust in their eyes, I reminded them of David's victory over the giant whose head, completely severed from the body, was on a table before me.

Everything is in order. The men had to be there when I broke the tomb, for I could not leave my only son in this world of death. Rather, I will take him with me; for being a man after my heart, David has done all my will. My son played every part that I have played while wearing the part of man. I would not leave my loved one in this world of death, so I broke the grave and resurrected him. Having redeemed him, I now take him into my heavenly state where - without speech - we share in each other's wisdom.

I urge you to condemn no one. No matter what he has ever done, you have done it, will do it, or are doing it now. Every part was created by the gods who came down and assumed human nature in order to play them all. That was our crucifixion.

I remember the night I led the procession to the house of God. I can still feel the ecstasy I knew as I became the six vortices - the Magen David, the great Star of David - and was sucked into and took upon myself the cross of man. Now, like Paul, I teach Christ as Imagination's power and wisdom, crucified. Christ is now in you because he has already been unified with the body you wear. And you will remember who you really are when you reenact the drama of scripture. If you really want to awaken, dwell upon what I have told you. I am not flattering you. You and I are the gods who came down. We are not less than we were before we came. We are greater for having descended and for redeeming this section of creation called man, but we cannot leave any section unredeemed. We have now proved that we can come into the world and overcome death, and we will redeem everything we created, in time. We created every state and loved it at the time of creation. And we will play every state before the quiescence of it all - our eternal beloved being called David, calls us Father. And you will take him with you, for he is your only begotten son who revealed you to yourself.

David died and was buried, but you will not leave him in the world of death. You will break the shell with a terrific explosion as though the skull erupts, and David - who was buried there - is set free to reveal you to yourself. Then, in time, you will take him back into the heavenly sphere, the eternal, the everlastingly enduring state of the redeemed.

Now let us go into the silence.

God's Almighty Power

G od's almighty power and wisdom expresses itself most characteristically in the acceptance of what the world calls weakness or foolishness.

Matthew tells the story of one who - Knowing himself to be the personification of God's creative power and wisdom - questions himself, saying: "If you are the Son of God, turn this stone into bread."[1] Then he quoted the 8th chapter of Deuteronomy, saying: "It is written, 'Man shall not live by bread alone, but by every word that proceeds out of the mouth of God.' "Here we discover that his hunger is no longer for bread made with flour, but for the hearing of the word of God, with understanding. The conflict recorded in this chapter is taking place in the mind of the individual, although it appears to be happening on the outside. Standing on the pinnacle, his adversary quoted the 91st Psalm, saying: "If you are the Son of God cast yourself down from here, for it is written, 'He will give his angels power to lift you up lest you dash your foot against a stone.'" Then, quoting the 6th chapter of Deuteronomy, he replied: "It is written, 'You shall not tempt the Lord your God.' "

In the third and final temptation he is shown all of the kingdoms of the earth and their glory, when the adversary said: "All of these are yours if you will bend down and worship me." Again, quoting the 6th chapter of Deuteronomy, he replies: "It is written, 'You shall worship the Lord your God and him only shall you serve.' "Then the adversary departs, and the great ministry begins. Who is the Lord your God, that you should worship and serve? Your own wonderful human imagination, he who is one with the God who created the world. The richest definition of God given

---

[1] *Matthew 4 -*

to us in scripture is: the Father of the Lord our God. I discovered I was God's son by experiencing scripture, but the son and God the Father are one!

Both the Father and the Son are defined as power, with wisdom added to the Son. In the Book of Mark, the high priest asked: "Are you the Christ, the Son of the Blessed?" and he replied, "I am, and you shall see the Son of man sitting at the right hand of Power." Power is capitalized in this passage, as it is the name given to God. In the Book of Luke, he is first called the Blessed, then Power, I am called the wisdom of God. Matthew tells of one who knows God has unfolded within him, and all of the characteristics of God as belonging to him - but he is puzzled and puts himself to the test. Scripture tells the story as though another being appears; but when God unveils himself, you question yourself, saying: if this is true, I should be able to do anything, for all things are possible to God. But I must not tempt the Lord. The only way is to trust him. So again, let me repeat: God's almighty power and wisdom expresses itself most characteristically in the acceptance of what the world calls weakness or foolishness.

When I was drafted, and we as a country were at war, in the eyes of the world I was foolish to believe that I could be honorably discharged without going to war. As far as the world was concerned, I was in for the duration, but I didn't want any part of it. I firmly believed that Jesus Christ was my own wonderful human imagination, that he was one with God, and that all things were possible to him. I knew I could not compel God to do anything. That He would act only as I imagined!

Trusting God, I slept as though I were honorably discharged and out of the army. I did everything in my mind's eye that I would do were it a physical fact, and fell asleep in that knowledge. Then, in vision, I saw my discharge paper with the word "Disapproved" crossed out and the hand of God write "Approved" above it in bold script. And when I heard the words: "That which I have done, I have done. Do nothing!" I did nothing. Nine days later I was honorably discharged and back in my home in New York City.

Remembering what I had done to get out of the army, when I was confronted with a similar problem a few years later, I applied the same principle to get out of the island of Barbados. Like Paul, I knew whom I have believed; so, when I was told I could not leave the island for months, I assumed once more that I am where I would like to be. I slept in the assumption it was true, and within hours the confirmation was mine. So you see, I know, from experimental faith, the one in whom I believe. You must believe in your human imagination and make him the rock upon which you stand. He is the Lord your God, and the only one whom you serve. If you are going to serve another, then you do not know God. If your boss tells you to do what he says and eventually you will get a raise, and your trust is in your boss, then you don't trust the Lord your God. Put your faith in anyone outside of your own wonderful human imagination and you don't trust God, for there is no other creative power!

If you put your trust in knowing the right people, having stocks and bonds, or money in the bank, you are trusting false gods. In 1925 I was in London, dancing for one hundred pounds a week. That was $480 U.S. dollars. We had an offer to go to Paris and on to Germany if we would accept payment in marks or francs, but we declined, for they were of no value. Their money was printed so fast, the paper was more valuable than that which was printed on it. I had traveled to London with a German family who were American by adoption. They had enormous securities in marks, and thought themselves very rich; but when we returned, they were poorer than church mice, as every cent they had was gone. Putting their trust in German marks was trusting a false god. Your boss is a false god. I don't care what it is - everything outside of self is false.

Now, after the third temptation we discover the mind is at peace, and there is no more conflict within. There is no devil, no

Satan - only doubts. Doubt, in the mind of one who was born by the grace of God, gives God the feeling of impossibility. In Blake's "Vision of the Last Judgment" he so wisely personified doubt, saying: "Satan thinks that sin displeases God. He ought to know that nothing displeases God but unbelief and eating of the tree of knowledge of good and evil."

Unless you believe you are the one you formerly believed to be up in heaven, and therefore outside of you, you will continue to miss your mark in life. Believing in himself when confronted by the last temptation, he said: "You shall worship the Lord your God, and him only shall you serve." Are you serving him? If so, things will come to pass, for there is no other channel that one can accept, other than confidence and trust in self! Believe in the Lord thy God one hundred per cent! If you need a certain amount of money and you have no collateral or anyone to turn to on the outside, will you trust the Lord your God to provide it for you? Knowing that all things are possible to God, will you turn to him in absolute confidence and trust, and mentally assume you had the money? Not being concerned as to how the money will come to you, will you test God's power and wisdom by falling asleep aware of having the money? If you will, you are serving God and in a way your surface mind could not devise, the money will be yours. Then, having tested the depths of your own being, you will know whom (not what) you have trusted. You will know whom you have believed. And that sure knowledge will vindicate your past trust. This is how God's wonderful principle works.

One night in New York City I was on the radio from midnight until 6:00 o'clock in the morning, with a panel of five men and one moderator. When I spoke of imagination creating reality, a professor said: "If that is true, turn this white pencil into a yellow one." I said: "All right. Bring me some yellow paint and I will do it." Wanting me to use my imagination and change the pencil instantly, I said: "You know, you are the scoffer of the Bible. I tell you, you shall not tempt the Lord your God." Then he questioned:

"Are you my God?" and I replied: "I didn't say that. You must find the Lord your God, because you are tempting him. You do not know it, because you haven't found him yet, but you will." Every child born of woman will reveal himself as the Son of God, and know he is God's power and wisdom. And since all things are possible to God, all things are possible to him. Then, confronting himself, when his adversary says: "Turn this pencil into a yellow one," he will imagine it yellow. If the pencil remains white when he thinks of it, he has not trusted the Lord. But if he persists in having a yellow pencil, by trusting the Lord completely, someone he may admire or does not want to offend, will give him a yellow one.

Whatever your desire may be, imagine it is fulfilled, and trust the Lord your God implicitly. If it takes a million people to play the part they must play in order to produce what you have assumed you are, they will do it. This is the world in which we live.

Jesus Christ is your own wonderful human imagination! Believe me. The Father's name is I AM. Everyone who can say I AM is God's image, yet there is only one God the Father! Learn to trust your I Amness and firmly believe in him, and you will know the day when the Lord shall be king over all the earth, and his name shall be one, and the Lord one! I have found the Lord of whom Moses and the law and the prophets wrote. I heard of him and learned to trust him, long before He unveiled himself in me in a series of events which belong only to the Son of God. Then I knew I was the identical being that the world worships on the outside, and calls Jesus Christ.

Men go to church and pray to a god who does not exist, when the only God makes man alive, for man could not breathe, were God not housed within him. So when you find God, trust him implicitly; but let me warn you: He will not accept your orders! Only as you imagine the wish fulfilled, will He act upon it. Tonight, as you put your head on that pillow, snuggle into the mood of the wish fulfilled in absolute confidence, and trust that God has ways and means your surface mind knows not of. I urge you to believe me, that you also may say with Paul: "I know whom I have believed." You will not fail, when you find the Lord your God, who is your own wonderful human imagination. You will learn to trust him completely. Knowing there is no need to help God by devising the means to fulfill your desire, you will move under compulsion, when the time for its fulfillment appears.

A lady I know took off to Paris with her two children, leaving her maid in charge of her apartment in New York City. When the lady returned, the apartment was empty, and the maid was nowhere to be found. The lady contacted the police, hired private detectives, and did everything humanly possible to find her furniture - to no avail. Then she came to me. We sat quietly in the silence and she returned to her apartment in her imagination. She walked through the rooms, feeling conscious of being there, now! She saw the furniture just as it had been before, touched the keys of her piano, and knew everything was back in place again.

A few days later, this lady went to her bank on Madison Avenue. Leaving the bank, she turned in the wrong direction and walked one block before she realized what she was doing. Looking down, she saw a familiar pair of ankles, and suddenly realized she had found her maid. As the light changed, she grabbed the girl and made her take her to where the furniture was stored. This lady now has her furniture back, every piece intact. All we did was trust the Lord our God. What would I have done to find the furniture for her, when the New York police or private detectives could not? But we trusted the Lord, our God. We didn't get down on our knees and plead for help, but simply sat in the silence and imagined. I assumed she was telling me she had found the furniture, and everything was in perfect order. When we broke the silence, I - trusting the Lord to bring it to pass - simply forgot it.

So I ask: who is the Lord who creates all things? I am! Scripture tells us that all things were made by the Lord, and without him was not anything made that was made. I know exactly what we did and I know what happened, therefore, I know exactly how it was made! Man finds it difficult to believe that such a power is housed within him. He reads the scripture: "Do you not realize that Jesus Christ, the power and wisdom of God who is one with God is in you?" and still bows before man-made little altars, and believes that someone on the outside is especially equipped to interpret God for him.

There are those who dare to claim that they are the sole deposit of the wisdom of God. What nonsense! God is housed in every child born of woman. But, being misled, man worships a false God, one who never existed and never will exist. There is no intermediary between you and God. Don't think of God with Jesus Christ as the intermediary between you and Him. There is only God! He became just as you are, that you may become as He is! This is the story.

The King James Version of the 20th chapter of the Book of Acts gives the true, literal translation of the Greek as: "By the blood of God we are redeemed." The RSV translated the word as "Lord", which always means "Jesus". But redemption comes from God. Becoming just as you are, with all of your weaknesses and limitations that you may become as He is, God redeems you, for you are his love! Trust God completely. He uses the weakness and foolishness of man, because the wisdom of this world is foolishness in his eyes. Men think themselves so wise. Rationalizing everything, man thinks he will find God one day on some planet or in a corner, but he never will. Man will go to the moon, the stars, and every place he desires, because whatever man can imagine, man can do!

Someone, today, who knows nothing of science, is dreaming fiction; and tomorrow the so-called scientific mind will devise the means to fulfill it, because God is the one who is writing the fiction and fulfilling it, and all things are possible to God. I urge you to dream your fiction and trust the Lord, your God implicitly that you, too, may say: "I know whom I have believed." Then let it happen, and it will.

Many years ago, my father and brother, Victor, went to see a spot overlooking the water on 35 acres, which is quite large on the island of Barbados. Three sisters lived in a home there, and sold their cattle to my father. At the time he mentioned he would be interested in purchasing their property if they should ever desire to sell. Then, turning to Victor, he said: "This would be the ideal spot for a hotel." A few years later the ladies decided to sell. One man with a great deal of money wanted those 35 acres very much, but was in Brazil the day my father - who had imagined owning it - bought it. Now a beautiful hotel is on that spot. It is very popular and always crowded winter and summer, all because my father had a dream and dared to trust the Lord his God, who he knew to be within himself.

My father would never go to church. He didn't like the minister at all. What wonderful stories we have of my father and the minister. One day the minister said to my father: "I am one of the chosen." My father looked at him and said: "I wouldn't have chosen you." He was just as brash as that with everything he did. He had no respect for the man. He never saw the inside of a church, except when we children were baptized. When my sixth brother was to be baptized - by this same minister - my father took two sea captains as godfathers. At the last moment the minister asked if the two gentlemen were Episcopalians, and when one claimed to be a Presbyterian and the other a Methodist, the minister informed my father that the child could not be baptized with these men as godfathers. With that my father said: "Give me my son. I will baptize him myself." He took the child out of the minister's arms, dipped his free hand in the water, sprinkled it on the child's face and said: "In the name of Jesus, your name is Fred" and walked out. And that's his name -Fred Goddard. That's the kind of man my father was and still is. Not a bone in his body lacked courage. He found the Lord as his own wonderful human imagination, so when he wanted something he simply imagined he had it, and walked in that knowledge.

I promise you, when you find the Lord and really trust him, you will know a peace you have never known before. You will never again bow before anything or anyone. Knowing that only your own wonderful human imagination is holy, He will be the only one you will ever serve!

Now let us go into the silence.

God Is Light

We are told in the 1st Epistle of John, the 1st chapter: "This is the message we have received from him and proclaim to you, that God is light and in him there is no darkness at all." Is this a figure of speech or a literal fact? I am telling you from experience: it is a literal fact, for God is light!

There are three very firm statements made in scripture defining God. God is light. God is love, and God is spirit. John tells us here that God is light, a light in which there is no darkness.

Now try to follow me closely. The final gift to man is God himself and God is a revealer. Man's knowledge of himself is based on his knowledge of the revealer. Scripture records what is said of the revealer. As he awakens in you, read scripture carefully and you will discover to what extent God has revealed himself to you.

Jesus makes this statement: "I am the light of the world; he who follows me will not walk in darkness, but will have the light of life." He is the light that lightens every man as he enters the world. Is this really true? Back in 1926 when I was twenty-one, I was visiting a friend in Larchmont, N.Y. He was the manager of a private club where several hundred boys and girls were gathered to dance. I did not join the group but retired early, turned on the nightlight, and began to read a book. The next thing I knew the sun was up, the light was still burning, and the opened book was lying on my chest. I knew from the page number that I had not read more than a page or two before I fell into a deep, deep trance, because the book had not been disturbed during that long period of maybe ten or twelve hours. I awoke to find myself cataleptic. My body seemed frozen, yet I was conscious of having returned from knowing myself to be an infinite sea of vibrant, liquid, living light. There was nothing but myself. I was the light of the universe and nothing, not one being, existed outside of me. No planet, no sun, no moon - only an infinite sea of light and I the light of the world. So, I can say from experience: I am the light of the world!

When God awakens within you (and he will) you too will know you are He who is the light of the world, and if God is light then you must be God! After this revelation happens in you, every claim made in scripture concerning God will begin to unfold from within, just like a tree in blossom. You will know that God is love, for you will stand in the presence of infinite love, embrace and become one with that body.

I am human. I am man, and yet I know I am infinite love. Since my embrace I have no other feeling but the body of love that embraced me. While I am here talking with you now I am wearing but a small portion of myself, just a spark of an immensity of my own fiery being. I know from experience that I help and teach more when I am asleep then when I am awake, for now when I sleep I pass beyond the world of dream into a world of spirit waking. I know from the thought, the imaginings, the visions I have received from many of you, that they are fiery darts shot from my own fiery self. That same being of love is waking within us all and when he wakes, for an interval you become the new lamp of the world. But your light is not here. It is beyond the world of dream for here, he who knows he is the light of the world is always rejected. "He came to his own and his own received him not." Even his own brothers did not believe in him. On this level it is always the same story, but when God awakens in you, you know who you are; and when the world calls you asleep, you are beyond the world of dream, having entered the world of Spirit waking; and from your fiery being you shoot your darts into the mind of those that you want to stir, to accept your message of salvation.

Now let me share with you this wonderful experience which was shared with me. In this lady's dream I was standing in the center of a raised platform, surrounded by many rows of people, all deformed in various ways. As I instructed them, one by one they were healed, then they rose and departed. Noticing a Madonna made of marble or stone nearby, she saw it become animated and dance for joy as the words I spoke so thrilled her. Then a few weeks ago she had this dream. In it I was a doctor in a hospital which had no surgery or drugs. Everyone simply came to me and was cured. Then she made this statement: "It is my hope that such a hospital can be here."

May I tell her: "No, it is not here on this level at all." This is a world of educated darkness where you and I - infinite beings as we are - entered for a purpose, and only a very small part of immortal self entered. That's what we see here. You are an infinite being, for you are God. Everyone is God, but here we are just a spark of the immensity of our own fiery being. And because ultimately we are one, when one awakens and passes beyond the world of dream, he fires his arrows into the minds of all to stir them, to set that spark ablaze so that everything said of Jesus Christ (God personified in scripture) will be experienced. When it happens in you, you don't need a new Bible or any credit on this level at all. You ask for no recognition. It was not granted then and it is not to be granted now. Even scripture tells us that even his own brothers did not believe in him. He came to his own people and they received him not. He was in the world and the world was made through him and the world knew him not. That is the story.

So much is said of light in scripture. He lights every man that comes into the world, because without his spark one could not breathe or live. God actually became us that we could become God, who is awakening and unfolding in all. One day you will know that you are all light, then all love, and finally all spirit. No mortal eye will ever see you, for although your birth from above does not appear in this world, the witnesses to the event are mortal. They see the sign of your birth, but they cannot see you because you are spirit. Talking about you as though you were not present, they speak of you in the most incredible terms saying: "How can he have a baby?" yet you take the sign in your arms and embrace it in the most endearing manner. That is the sign of your spiritual birth, revealing yet another definition that God is spirit.

Knowing that God is love and light, when your spiritual birth appears you will have experienced the three definitions of God. Then, still finding yourself confined to this little tiny portion of yourself, you will teach and help others in this world. Ask for no acclaim, no recognition, nothing - just simply teach it, and night after night as you fall asleep you will pass beyond the world of dream, and from the world of spirit waking you will shoot your fiery arrows into the minds of those who follow you. You will stir them and they will awaken as you have been awakened. At some time in your life you heard the story and, as you slept in the world of dream someone who knew God from experience shot an arrow into your mind and your spirit became a flame and God awoke in you. It's the same being, for there is no race in God, no sect, no color; it's just God and He is light.

We speak of darkness and light, yet is darkness a thing - or is it the absence of a thing? Is the hole in a sock a thing or is it the absence of a portion of the sock? I am speaking of actual light - vibrant, living, pulsing light, which hasn't a thing to do with the pigment of skin. I wear all garments - black, yellow, pink and red. I am not greater in one garment than I am in another. In Christ there is no Greek, no Jew, no bond, no free, no male, no female. God is one in all and He awakens in all, and when he does everything claimed of Jesus Christ is experienced. One day, having played the central part, you too will close your eyes and leave this world. Having shot your arrows well, those who heard and believed you will awaken. They may forget you in time that doesn't really matter, for the eternal story is recorded in the gospel. Your name may not be recorded there but it is recorded in eternity, for your true identity is God Himself!

On this level you can start from here, right now, and fulfill any dream. May I tell you: you are going to live the life that you are imagining, so imagine well! Imagine the most glorious thing in the world and - no matter how wonderful it is - may I tell you it is nothing compared to the being that you really are. Nothing in this world can come close to the being you really are. This world of Caesar is only a tiny section of your infinite being, but while you are here, dream nobly. Dream lovely dreams, for you can realize everything if you are willing to imagine that you have them now. Begin now to imagine you are the man (the woman) you would like to be, and regardless of what happens tomorrow, next week, or next month, if you persist in the assumption that you already are that which you want to be, you will become it in this world of flesh and blood. Everything here will vanish, yes - but why not test your creative power? Then you will begin to taste the power latent within you, and you will discover that you can conjure out of your own depth things that are seemingly impossible, conjured by the mere act of assumption. If you dare to act and persist in acting as though it were true and it becomes a fact, then you will know the truth of your creative power.

The promise you will have to take on faith. I tell you from experience: it is true. I have experienced the fact that God is love, the fact that God is the Father. Who would have thought that one born in 1905 (and my friend who is here tonight - in 1911) with no social, intellectual or financial background, would experience the fact that we are God the Father. That God's Son David - he who decreed: "I will tell of the decree of the Lord. He said unto me: 'Thou art my Son, today I have begotten thee'" - is our Son. Who would have thought that we, born in the 20th century, are the Father of one who was supposed to have lived 1000 BC, when we have no memory beyond that little moment in time. I can return to the age of three in my memory, yet we both returned to the same memory and remembered one who supposedly lived 3000 years ago.

We know from experience that we are the ones who declared: "You are my son, today I have begotten you." We know we are the immortal being who took upon ourselves mortality to test our own infinite power by becoming just a small part of it. Having played the various parts we agreed to play, Fatherhood once more has become a part of our consciousness, and David has stood before us and called us Father. This is the thrill that is in store for everyone.

So, when my friend saw this healing she saw correctly, for in 1946 I was lifted up, and as a heavenly chorus sang: "Neville is risen. Neville is risen," everyone before me was made perfect in harmony with the perfection springing from within me. That is in store for everyone in this world, and in the end we are all gathered into one being, yet without a loss of identity. There is a friendship and, as with friends, you accept the existence of others, so God's name is plural. It is a unity made up of others.

When you and I deliberately entered the state called Abraham we were told: "For a surety, your descendants will be sojourners in a land that is not theirs and they will be enslaved there for four hundred years. Then they will come out with great possessions." Four hundred is the last letter of the Hebrew alphabet, whose symbol is a cross. Now crucified on a garment of flesh, you are enslaved by it and must perform all of its normal, natural functions. Regardless of whether you are a king or a serf, you must perform all of the functions of man. Isn't that a slave? But one day "I" who am God will bring my identity with me, out of limitation and darkness into the world of light, for I am bringing out myself. It was God who made the decision and God who fulfills it in this wonderful world.

We are told in the 82nd Psalm: "I say, 'You are gods, sons of the Most High, all of you, nevertheless you will die like men and fall as one man, O princes.'" If you are a prince, is your father not a king? Coming out from the Father into the land of forgetfulness, memory died as we fell as one man. But when we return we are the king, for we return as the Father. Now Sons of the Most High, God's final gift to us is himself, and God is Love. God is Spirit and God is Light! And you are destined to experience everything that is claimed of Jesus Christ in the gospel.

Don't try to change the Bible - leave it just as it is. I stand amazed, yet I cannot be disturbed when I read how the great scholars interpret it. Today I took the word "light" and was amazed how the scholars interpreted it as a figure of speech. They could not believe the word could be taken in a literal sense, so they gave it every kind of interpretation. These are the great minds of the day, men who are masters of the ancient tongue, but they know nothing because they haven't had the experience. I tell you scripture is literally true. All the precepts of Jesus Christ must be accepted literally, for they will be experienced literally, in a region so remote from that which man knows or can even conceive. You can't even think of it here but God does it there, and you will know that you are the central character of scripture, as the whole thing unfolds within you.

On this level, you dwell on what I have told you this night. You will find that it will pay off in tremendous dividends. You will reach the point when you will know that your wish is already fulfilled. Then you will sigh and say: "Thank you Father." Even though you know you are the Father you can still address him as another, but an intimate self. "He who sent me is with me, he has never left me. If you see me you see him who sent me, for we are one. I and my Father are one." You can actually have a wish, thank him, and wait for it to appear in this world - and it will.

Now, the same lady who wrote the letter concerning the healing said: "I wanted to see Bergman, so I called the agencies. I called friends whom I thought had influence; I made every physical effort to obtain a ticket to no avail. Then, aggravated with myself, I simply assumed I was in the audience, watching the show and enjoying it thoroughly. A few days later a friend who lives in New York City called to ask if I could see him on a certain night, as he was going to be in town. I agreed and after dinner he took me to see Bergman."

This lady made every physical effort to get a seat, but not one was available. Yet when she assumed she was there, three thousand miles away a friend decided to come west and take her. Now, people will tell you that tickets are available out of town, or that certain seats are kept aside for special people, for people are forever justifying everything. But my friend didn't ask for justification, she simply assumed she was seated in the theater and a friend three thousand miles away fulfilled her imaginal act.

You can be anything you want to be, for you are going to be what you are imagining anyway. As man imagines, he lives! Morning, noon, and night you can't stop imagining, because the candle has been lit. Job tells us that the spirit of the Lord is the candle on his head. Your candle is now lit and you are moving through a world of darkness towards the fulfillment of all that you have imagined; so, imagine the best, for everything is yours for the taking. Fulfill every desire while you are here, and when you come to the end you will discover that you are God. You began as God and you end as God, for "I am the beginning, and the end, the first and the last, the alpha and the omega." God can't bring out another, so out of himself comes all that goes to make God, for he is the *elohim*, a compound unity. In the beginning God (*elohim*) is one made up of others. You and I came out of the *elohim* and in the end we go back as the *elohim*, but this time we are aware of being the Father. As common sons (princes) we return as the king. That is the journey for everyone in this world.

I am telling you from experience, the story is true. God is light. In the Book of 1 John, he speaks as though he had only heard and not yet experienced, saying: "We will tell what we have heard from him and proclaim to you that God is light and in him there is no darkness at all." But in the Gospel of John, he speaks from experience and puts these words in the mouth of the central character, saying: "I am the light of the world. He who follows me will not be in darkness, for I am the light of life." Here we see light identified with life. There is something within you which is all light, the light of life by which you animate and start things moving, just as the lady saw the statue. It was dead, made of marble; but as everyone was perfectly formed, the Madonna became animated and began to dance. You animate everything, for you are God, buried in your mortal body, which is an eternal part of the universe. The bodies you see here are sepulchers. They appear to be alive while you wear them, but they are dead. You animate them, for you are the princes who - dwelling as one man - became fragmented into all these little parts. The one who fell was the king. Now a prince, you are gathering yourself together into the one being called the Lord God Jehovah, who is Jesus Christ.

I know it doesn't make sense on this level. It is not expected to, but I tell you it is true. Night after night I go to bed and move beyond the world of dreams into the world of spirit making, and from there I shoot my fiery arrows, knowing they never miss. Then someone will bring me a message, telling me she saw circles after circles after circles in the air and an arrow penetrate the smallest circle and swivel. She brought back an image, for that is exactly what happens. The arrow never misses its target. The message always penetrates and sets aflame that which is already there. So I tell you: your imaginings, your dreams, your visions, are fiery arrows shot by a being who is all light!

Now let us go into the silence.

God's Creative Power

We are told in the Book of Exodus: "God said to Moses, 'I AM the I AM. I appeared to Abraham, to Isaac, and to Jacob as God Almighty, but by my name I AM I did not make myself known to them.'" And if you read the 1st chapter, the 24th verse of 1 Corinthians, you will discover that the I AM (the creative power of God) is personified as Jesus Christ! Now you and I are called upon to find this creative power. The Christian world claims to believe in Christ, but they do not know him for he must be found. This challenge is given in scripture. "Examine yourselves to make sure you are holding to the faith. Test yourselves!" If you want to find Jesus Christ you must test yourself!

Are you really convinced that Jesus Christ is in you? Have you tested him? If you have and are still not sure, then you have failed the test. Ask the highest leader of the Christian faith down to the lowest if he believes that Jesus Christ is in him, and if he is not convinced that the creative power of the universe is within and personalized as himself, then he has failed to meet the test regardless of what his man-made rank may be. You can attend all the churches in the world, give to the sick and poor on the outside, but if you do not know from experience that Jesus Christ is in you, you have failed the test. I tell you that Jesus Christ is your own wonderful human imagination, who is the eternal creative power of God. If you do not know that, you do not know Jesus Christ! You may say: "He is a person." Well, you are a person, aren't you?

Jesus Christ is God the Father and God the Father is Spirit, and those who worship him do so in Sprit through the art of feeling! I have imagined a state and seen it externalize itself and become a physical fact that I may share with another. This I have done unnumbered times and taught others to do it. So, I have found him and know him to be the only creative power of the universe. Everything in your world which is now a fact to be shared with others was once only imagined. And if you know that Jesus Christ is the creative power that brings things into this world, that all things must be first imagined, then you have found him. Having found him, you must learn to trust him and live by this principle. Do this and you will find yourself moving into the stream of eternal life by fulfilling scripture and knowing that "All power in heaven and earth is given unto me."

The true meaning of power is "effectiveness in achieving a purpose." Today as a nation we have the power of the atom bomb, but are not willing to use it because it is not our objective to wipe out cities; so where is the power that could bring about our purpose? Man does not know Jesus Christ, therefore he thinks there is power in nuclear energy, in money, in his intellectual or social position; but the only power is Jesus Christ who is the human Imagination!

I was born and raised in a Christian environment, yet I did not learn this truth in Sunday school, in church, or at home. I was taught to believe in a being outside of myself. Some person who was born two thousand years ago who was crucified on a wooden cross by people who did not believe he was the Son of God. This is the story my mother taught me as her mother had taught her. The story comes down this way, yet it is not the true story of scripture.

I tell you a mystery: Christ in you is the hope of glory, for God, your human imagination became man that man may become God. This is a mystery that we are called upon to test, for the power that created the world became as you are, that you may know yourself to be all creative power, as He is! I did not receive this knowledge from a man. I did not read it in a book, nor did I ever hear of it from another. It was revealed to me that God, in man, is his own wonderful human imagination!

Having no place to turn, or no one to turn to, I began to experiment; and as it proved itself in the testing, I found myself fulfilling scripture. Instead of another, I was playing the central role fulfilling the only belief! Then I began to tell it and those who heard and believed began to test themselves, and as they did, they moved into the mainstream and scripture fulfilled itself in them.

We are told: "Remain in the city until you are clothed with power from on high." Scripture personifies this fantastic power as Jesus Christ, but man is taught that Jesus Christ is some distinct individual outside of himself and turns to him to grant his wishes and respond to his prayers. Then one day man hears who Jesus Christ really is, and turning to no one on the outside, God reveals himself to that man as I AM. God said to Moses: "I made myself known unto Abraham, to Isaac, and to Jacob as God Almighty, but by my name I AM I did not make myself known to them."

If God's name forever and forever is I AM, how can you look outside of self? You cannot point to another and say: "I AM." You can observe this or do that, but you cannot point to another when you say:" I am."

Having revealed himself as Almighty Power, then I AM, God's third revelation, is that of Father. And if God is a Father, he must have a Son. The world has been taught to believe that Jesus Christ is God's Son, but I know from revelation that Jesus Christ is God Himself. There is a son, however, as told us so clearly in the 2nd Psalm. That son is David, who says: "I will tell of the decree of the Lord. He said unto me, 'Thou art my son, today I have begotten thee.'" I tell you scripture does not record secular history, but supernatural history. Its message is sacred and hasn't a thing to do with anything that took place in a secular manner.

Yesterday I read where someone in Ohio, who claimed he had traced his background back to David, died at the age of 84 or 85. Of all the nonsense of the world, if he meant it secularly. David is not a character of human history, but the eternal state one enters when he believes in God's power as his own imagination, exercises it, and enters the mainstream and awakens. Personifying God's creative power, David will stand before you and call you Father, revealing you to be one with your creative power.

Listen to these words carefully: "The high priest said to Jesus, 'Are you the Christ, the Son of Blessed?' And Jesus answered, 'I am, and you will see the son of man sitting at the right hand of Power.'" This he said in fulfillment of the 100th Psalm: "The Lord said unto my lord, 'Sit at my right hand till I make your enemies your footstool.'" Here we see Power equated with a man! So, God's first revelation is that of sheer power. Then comes his name, I AM, which is followed by his true character, which is that of a Father who loves.

It is God's purpose to give himself to everyone, and - being a Father - when he gives himself to you he gives you Fatherhood. First, he gives you Power, then the awareness of being that power as you test yourself.

Now I ask you to examine yourself. When confronted with a problem, do you turn to someone on the outside for its solution, or do you believe that all power resides in your human imagination? Do you believe in the hydrogen bomb, meeting the right people, or living on the "right" side of the street? Or do you believe in your own wonderful human imagination? I have found he of whom Moses and the law wrote, Jesus of Nazareth, to be my human imagination and I turn only to him for the solution of my problems. I do it by asking myself what I would see if my problem dissolved and its solution rose in its place. What would I hear? How would I act? Having discovered Jesus to be my imagination, I act as though the problem was solved, and have found from experience that I have brought things not seen by mortal eye into the world to be seen by all. I have proved it and encourage everyone to try it. Examine yourself to make sure, really sure, that you have completely accepted Jesus Christ as your human imagination, so that when confronted by any challenge you turn to the only Jesus Christ and not to a false one. If you turn to anyone outside of yourself you have turned to a false Jesus Christ and failed the test.

Turn only to God and not to anyone or anything on the outside. No one can tell your future, for your future is to fulfill Scripture, and you have no other!

I received a letter last week from a lady, who said: "In the dream I knew I was twenty years old, just married, and living in the Basque country among the shepherds. My husband was driving an old truck. I sat next to him with my sister-in-law next to me. In the rear sat my brother-in-law with my father-in-law directly behind me. Having spent the night on a mountain top, we travel over dusty, rugged mountainous roads as I become very tired and weak. My father-in-law had authority over everything, and knowing the way, he said: 'Just one more curve and we will be home.' As the final curve is completed I see a heavenly valley covered with green grass and a sparkling, crystal-clear river flowing through it. In the distance I see a beautiful home with barns and flocks of white sheep. Two shepherds are there with their crooks, their dogs, and a flock of geese. Then I turn around, and as I face my father-in-law I see he has suddenly grown tall and young. As I look at him I remember having seen that face somewhere in the dim, dim eternity. Then the face became brilliant and as I dissolved into the brilliance, I awoke."

In this letter my friend played the part of Tamar, as told us in the 38th chapter of the Book of Genesis. Judah, the fourth son of Jacob, is listed in the genealogy of Jesus Christ: "Abraham begat Isaac, Isaac begat Jacob, Jacob begat Judah and his brothers." In the story, Judah left his brothers, married outside, and had three sons. Choosing Tamar for his first son, Er, who displeased Jehovah and was killed, Judah told his second son to marry her and raise offspring for his brother. Knowing that every offspring would not be his, but his brother's, Onan spilled his seed so that Tamar would not have a child. Displeasing Jehovah because of this act, Jehovah killed him, for the command was to be fruitful and multiply and increase the world. The third son was not given as he was too young.

Then came the day when Judah went down to observe the shearing of the sheep, as he was rich and had enormous flocks. Tamar, upon hearing of his visit, took off her widow's clothes and sat in a public place, veiled as a harlot of the temple. When Judah proposed, she asked: "What will you give me?" and he replied: "A kid from my flock." Asking for a pledge that the kid would be sent, he gave her his ring, his bracelet, and his staff, and knew her intimately. Three months later it was brought to Judah's attention that his daughter-in-law, Tamar, was pregnant. When Judah heard the news, he said: "Let the law be fulfilled. She shall be burned to death." When they came to execute the law she took the ring, the bracelet, and the staff and sent them to Judah with the message: "The man who gave me these is the father of the child." Upon seeing them, Judah said: "The sin is mine, not hers,"

Now don't think of Tamar as having union in a physical sense, but union with a state, for every time we enter a state there is union. In my friend's vision, everyone present was an in-law, telling her that she has entered the mainstream. She has had union with memory, and no power on earth can stop her from bringing scripture to its fulfillment, for her father-in-law is the one spoken of in the 49th chapter of Genesis as "the lion's whelp, and from his hand the scepter will never pass." She has entered the state which leads her up to the climax as Jesus Christ, who is God the Father!

The day will come when you will reach the Fatherhood degree and David will stand before you and call you Father. Then you will know a power that is greater than the human mind can fathom. You will know real power. It hasn't a thing to do with the ability to destroy a nation. Tonight we could release X number of bombs and destroy every city in Russia and they could do the same thing to us - so what? May I tell you: the millions who would die on both sides would not be dead, but still trying to find the Father! Everyone is really searching for the Father of all life, and that Father is Jesus Christ. Although men have created pictures of him, Jesus is not on the outside. We are told: "It does not yet appear what he shall be, but we know that when he appears, we shall be like him, for we shall see him as he is." God's son cannot appear and not be just like the person to whom he appears. You will never see him as someone coming from without but coming from within you. He will call you father in the Spirit and then you will know who you really are!

In the meanwhile you can exercise your power on this level if you will accept this challenge. Examine yourselves and make sure you are faithful to your imaginal act! Let no one else examine you, but test yourself! Have you completely accepted the fact that Jesus Christ is in you? If you can answer, "not quite" then you have failed the test. If, like one billion Christians, you believe in some other Jesus Christ, you have a false Christ. And you will never find him by going to church or giving to the poor, for he is not on the outside, but in your own wonderful human imagination!

Let no one prophesy for you! The only prophecy you are destined to fulfill is scripture. When someone tries to tell me what some astrologer or medium said I get so annoyed I want to shout: "Have you ever heard me?" Believe in all that nonsense, and you worship false Christs! If you want to be famous in this world of men, use this principle and you will shine for your little moment, but I ask you: are you in the mainstream of fulfilling scripture? Do you really believe in the only Jesus Christ, who is your human imagination? I say: there never was another Christ and there never will be another Christ.

Now, some will say that is blasphemy, just as they did long ago. In the 14th chapter of the Book of Mark, the question is asked: "Are you the Christ?" And Jesus said: "I am; and you will see the Son of man sitting at the right hand of Power." Then the high priest said: "Do we still need witnesses? You have heard his blasphemy." And in the Book of John, when accused of blasphemy "because you, being man, make yourself God" Jesus said: "Is it not written in your law, 'I say, you are gods'? If scripture says you are gods, and scripture cannot be broken, is it blasphemy for me to say

I am the Son of God, and the Son and the Father are one?" If you are creative power, you must be one with the creator, who is a person as you are, as I am.

So I say to everyone: accept Christ as your own wonderful human imagination and don't falter, for scripture must be fulfilled in you. It is not done physically! I have experienced a physical birth, for I was born in Barbados and just as you, I know the limitations of the flesh. I came into this world with nothing and do not have much today. But because I didn't have much, I had to stand upon my own two feet and believe in myself. Asking no one to help me and not stealing from another, if I had nothing I went without it. I have seen those who had more than they needed, but I didn't take it from them, I simply pulled in my belt. I have walked fifty blocks to find a friend who had a dime to buy some soup beans. When he could not be found I would return and perhaps the next day earn a quarter to buy the beans, but it never occurred to me that because others had food and I didn't that they should give it to me. I was determined to believe in myself and because of that I got into the mainstream of life and scripture began to unfold in me. No one owes me a living; all I have to do is trust Jesus Christ, trust my human imagination!

I have no desire to pile up a lot of money. Why pile up a million shadows? My desire is to tell you who Jesus Christ really is. He is your own wonderful human imagination. There never was another Christ and there never will be another. If you will trust him - and I use "him" advisedly because God's creative power and God is a person (and you are that person) - you will never fail, for he will never fail you! Tonight, if you know what you want, just believe that you have it. Sleep as though it were true, and because Christ is in everyone, he will use as many as necessary to aid the birth of your assumption.

In the end of the Bible, the 22nd chapter of Revelation, Jesus Christ is speaking, saying: "I am the root and the offspring of David, the bright morning star." And in the 2nd chapter of the same book it is said: "To he who conquers" (who witnesses the truth of scripture) I will give the morning star." In other words, he gives you himself as God the Father. He is the root of David. The root of a tree is its father. God the Father is the root of David, for David is all Spirit, not a being of flesh and blood. He is the eternal state of the Son, who calls everyone to come to the mainstream and climax as the Father. So the story ends when you have finished the race and kept the faith, for you are given the morning star and know yourself to be the root and the offspring of David, the bright morning star!

Tonight, test yourself! I will not test you. I am not here to test anyone. I only urge you to examine yourself to see if you are really keeping the faith, or are you going to call a friend and tell him how horrible things are and appeal to him on the outside? I ask you: are you really keeping the faith? Do you always turn to your imagination and, no matter what happens, do you remain faithful to the state imagined? If you do, you have passed the test. But if every little rumor, doubt, or fear can move you around like a pawn on a chessboard, then you are not keeping the faith! It's entirely up to you. Are you testing yourself or not? Can you say within yourself: "I always turn to my imagination when confronted with a problem and solve it there. Then I remain faithful to that imaginal act." If you can, you have passed the test. It's just as simple as that.

May I tell you: we remain in this world of death until we enter the mainstream and come to the climax. You can't believe how much this world is really a world of death, whose life is in you as your human imagination. Life itself is an activity of imagining where everything is a symbol. Your closest, dearest friend, your wife, your mother, father, brothers and sisters are all symbols, all dead symbols revealing to you who you really are.

Now let us go into the silence.

God Speaks To Man

"In a vision of the night when deep sleep falls upon men, while they slumber on their beds, he opens their ears and seals their instructions."[2]

Tonight you may find yourself in a terrestrial world like this one, and you feel just as real to yourself as you do here. And when you return with its memory you may think it was a dream, but it was a vision. You are dreaming right now, for this world is the dream you and I agreed to complete. Its end will appear when we turn around through a series of visions.

The Old Testament outlines the dream, interspersed with vision, while the New Testament tells of the awakening. The trinity which the churches refer to as God the Father, God the Son and God the Holy Spirit, can be taken in a simple way as Mighty Father, the proceeding Son, and the returning Holy Spirit - for they are all one.

The dreamer in you is God. Tonight, as you dream ask yourself where you are. Many times while lying on my bed I have left this body I know so well, to enter a world just as real as this. Remembering where my body was when I started my journey, when I desired to return I had to feel myself in the body - now cataleptic - on the bed. I could not move it or open its eyes. The body felt dead, yet I was very much alive. Gradually I was able to move a finger, then the toes. But only as I opened my eyes and saw the familiar objects on the wall and dresser did I know I was back. But was I really? Am I not dreaming this world just as much as I was dreaming that one? If so then where am I right now?

---

[2] *Job 33 -*

Man cannot remember where he laid himself down to dream this dream of life. If he could, he would return through the secret of feeling. Finding myself in a world like this, I remembered where I left my body and felt myself back into it. I returned with the memory of people who were there. They were clothed and real and the world was terrestrial, just as it is here. I talked to them and they answered. Now if that world was a vision then this one is also, for one world does not differ from the other. So God has two ways of speaking to man, but man does not perceive it.

A dream contains one central thought. Like a thank you note. You don't try to interpret every word in it, just the message it is trying to convey.

I have a friend who dreamed it was his birthday and many people had arrived to attend his party. There were two large cakes, with one lady very adamant about the design she had placed on hers. (This is not significant to the dream, but only part of getting the story started.) Leaving to find candles for the table, my friend returned to discover one cake was missing, as well as all of the guests. Disappointed because he had not seen or heard me speak, the dream ended. Suddenly he finds himself on a beach with a friend. Asking where everyone was, his friend points to a rock in the middle of the water, and said: "There they are, away out to sea." Seeing another rock near it supporting a child, afraid and alone, he said: "How did they get there?" and his friend answered: "Mentally." Then he mentally went to the child, took her by the hand, and placed her on the big rock. Now the dream changes and my friend finds himself in a lecture hall with a stairway in the center of the stage. Coming down the stairs, I place his hands in mine and say: "I'm glad you have made it, chosen one." Then he awoke.

This is a very significant dream; whose single jet of truth is the rock. It's not the birthday, the party, or the cake, but the language of scripture that will reveal the truth of any dream. The journey of life is a mental one, which is taking place in the sea of illusion. And only when you find yourself on the Rock will your journey be at its end.

We are told: "You are unmindful of the Rock that begot you and have forgotten the God who gave you birth."[3] This passage of scripture tells us that the Rock is equated with God. And in the New Testament it is said: "They drank from the supernatural Rock that followed them and the Rock was Christ."

This gentleman is now standing on that Rock. Since all dreams are egocentric, he conjured me from within himself Containing the whole vast world within him, he called forth those he chose to play a part he wrote for himself. This he did without our knowledge or consent. My friend has now reached that foundation stone upon which he will build his house. No longer will he build on shifting sands, where the winds and storms destroy the structures, but upon the Rock who is Christ; and Christ is God who is the Human Imagination.

The central figure of Christianity is the Human Imagination. When you accept this as the first principle of religion, then all governments, rituals, and external worship will have heard the trumpets of Joshua. All of the buildings that are of any structure than that Rock - which is your own wonderful Human Imagination - will fall. This gentleman had a wonderful experience. He is on the Rock, but he may move from it. He may turn his back and forget that the cause of all of the phenomena of his life is the Human Imagination. It is my hope that he will not.

There is only one source of all creation. "By him all things were made, and without him was not anything made that was made." If anything, or anyone comes into your world, remember the cause is your Human Imagination, who is the God of scripture and the dreamer in you.

Stand upon that Rock, knowing you are God the Father, the Son, and the Holy Spirit, as these three are the chosen One. In the

---

[3] *Deuteronomy 32 -*

1st Epistle of John, the 5th chapter, these three are called the Spirit, the water, and the blood.

Knowing that God is spirit and there is life in the blood, the Risen Christ calls himself the Living Water, saying: "If you had asked, I would have given you living water that you would never thirst again." Living water is the truth. Once truth has been experienced, you will hunger and thirst no more. "I will send a famine upon the land. It will not be a hunger for bread or a thirst for water, but for the hearing of the word of God." This gentleman has found the word of God, for he has found the Rock.

Another friend shared this vision with me. (I call this a vision rather than a dream, for it was her own back door.) Although it was early in the day, my friend became so sleepy, she lay down on the couch and closed her eyes. Suddenly she heard a knock at the back door. Upon opening it she found a pleasant looking young man there, obviously hungry. She invited him in and as she was preparing his food, she realized it was 5:30 P.M. and her husband would be home shortly. Wondering how she was going to explain the stranger's presence, her little daughter woke her, to discover that it was only 11:00 a.m. in the morning. Lying there she remembered she had not fed the man, so she did so in her Imagination.

That's what I mean when I tell you to carry Imagination to the extreme point and feed the world. Although my friend did not feed the man in her vision, she did so in her Imagination, knowing she was feeding Christ. She knows that when she does this to the least of one of these, she is doing it to Christ. And when she does not do it, she is not doing it to Christ - who is her very self. My friend has learned her lesson, and is at the end of her journey. Having a vivid memory of what had transpired, she carried through her intention and fed the man in her Imagination.

All of this may seem insane to the world, because they do not understand this great mystery. In 1946 I wrote a little booklet called The Search. I ended it on this note: "The universe which we study with such care is a dream and we the dreamers, dreaming non-eternal dreams. One day, like Nebuchadnezzar, we shall awaken from our nightmare in which we fought with demons, to discover that we have never really left our eternal home; that we were never born and have never died - save in our dream."

Since that time nothing has happened to cause me to change one word in that little book for, like Nebuchadnezzar, I have awakened from this dream of life. Now when I close my eyes in meditation, I sometimes have a little dream; or other times I enter a world just like this, where I am totally awake and aware of what is happening.

You see, one day the being that is really dreaming your life will awaken, and you will be enhanced beyond your wildest dreams because of your experiences.

You never descended in body, but in consciousness. Descending in your dream, you entered this world called eternal death to see things appear, wax, wane, and vanish. They appear to die, yet you are dreaming their death. One day you will discover that you have never gone anywhere, save in your dream.

This past weekend I was visiting with a doctor, who told me that he was fascinated with anthropology, and if he ever came back again, he was going to be an anthropologist. He said: "Neville, in spite of what you say, we go back millions and millions of years." And I asked: "Are you proud of the fact that your ancestor was an ape? If all ends run true to origin, and your ancestor was an ape, no matter how wise you are, you are still only a wise ape. Well, my origin is God. I assumed this limitation for a purpose, and when that purpose is revealed, my end is God."

I cannot see any relationship between the physical body and the ape, as there are still apes with us. Did it ever occur to you that change does not need to be gradual, but can be a combination in a sudden mutation? Think about it. God is a dreamer. He could take a root or a branch, and by forcing mutation among members of a certain colony of apes, when they multiply the new feature is transferred, and man suddenly appears.

Man thinks in terms of millions and millions of years; yet one generation could be more instantaneous than the nth part of a second, if you are going to measure life in terms of time.

I'm not saying this is true. I am only giving you something to think about. If you do, you will change your mind about having an ape for an ancestor.

As God, you started your dream by coming down in consciousness to the level called man. You died in order for humanity to be made a living soul. Now, bound by what you took upon yourself, you are dreaming a predetermined, horrible dream; yet the results of these experiences will transcend your wildest dreams. The story of Jesus Christ is your story, which you will fulfill - in vision - in a three-dimensional world.

Now, I used the word mutation for a purpose. We are told that at the end: "In the twinkle of an eye, our lowly bodies will be changed to be one form with His glorious body." This does not take time. The moment you are embraced by the Risen Lord, your lowly body is transformed to be one form with His glorious body of light, of love, and wisdom. These bodies of flesh and blood cannot inherit the kingdom of God. You need an entirely different body to function in that age. That body is a mutation, as it comes suddenly.

When I stood in the presence of the Risen Christ I was asked to define the greatest thing in the world. I answered with the words of Paul, "Faith, hope, and love, these three, but the greatest of these is love." Then Infinite Love embraced me. We fused and I became one with the Risen Lord.

There is no creative power comparable to love! I know, for I am one with that body; and when this aspect of myself is called dead, I will wear that body, for my dream is over. Then you can say of me what Shelley said of one who had departed: "He has awakened from the dream of life. `Tis we who, lost in stormy vision, fight with phantoms, an unprofitable strife."

Everyone will awaken from this dream to know he is love; for there is nothing but God and God is love. The most horrible being is God, as the most glorious. In the end, when the curtain comes down, we will collectively form the one Man, the one Spirit, the one Body. Then we will understand why we conceived the dream and played it, as we will have expanded into a further existence as a result of this experience of coming down into the world of eternal death.

I know that when I have entered other sections of time, in vision, the experience was real, just as this is now. The world may say my experience was just a dream. But if this is reality and that just as real as this, then this is a dream. The difference is that when I was there, I remembered where my body was and was able to return to it.

Could you remember the being you were before you started this dream of life, and use the same technique, you would feel yourself there and vanish from sight to awaken in that body.

For myself, I have worn that wakened body since 1929, when I was embraced by the Risen Lord. At that time we became the one body, one Spirit, one Lord, one God and Father of all, who is above all, through all, and in all. I have heard Him say: "I laid myself down within you to sleep, and as I slept I dreamed a dream. I dreamed..." and I knew exactly what He was saying: "I am dreaming I am Neville."

One day you will know that the visions of the day are no more real than those of the night, for you will know you are their reality. You will realize that you cannot encounter strangers, regardless of whether they be harmful or helpful, as they came out of you to play the part you had already played from within.

The world and all of its conflicts appear to show us that Imagination can and does run amok. Imagination is the only foundation. It is the Rock upon which one builds his house. No matter what happens, blame no one, but remain on that Rock; for Christ (your own wonderful Human Imagination) is He, and the only cause of the phenomena of life. Accept this truth and you will have a firm foundation upon which to build.

As you dwell upon this power vested in you, you will discover it will help you far beyond your wildest dreams. You will realize that you do not need the help of anyone. All you need do is assume you have what you want. Then dare to walk in that assumption; and if it takes a thousand people to aid its birth, they will appear and play their parts, not knowing why or what they do. They will do it without their permission or consent, just as I did in my friend's dream.

Man prays to an outside Jesus and believes in an outside God, because he has forgotten the God who gave him birth. Scripture tells us that when Moses revealed the true God as I AM, he hadn't been gone more than moments when the people once more turned and worshipped the golden cow as the cause of their fortunes, good or bad. They started worshipping things made with the human hand in violation of the eighth commandment: "Make no graven image unto me," either with your hands or in your mind!

If you see a Jesus Christ as other than your own wonderful Human Imagination, you have made a graven image. But when you find the true Christ - called the Rock - and start building on it, no rumors or arguments can knock your house down. Build on the sand and your house will slip away, but if you create your world believing in your own wonderful Human Imagination - called Jesus Christ - nothing will destroy it.

Your Imagination is Christ, dreaming in you and creating your world. Feed him noble thoughts. Become selective and dare to assume something wonderful for yourself. Our newspapers are telling us how to transcend death and live to be one hundred, adding years to life - yet no one thinks of adding life to years!

Schubert lived only thirty-one years, yet he gave us a thousand pieces of music. Keats died at twenty-six. So many of the great poets died young but look what they gave us! They didn't add years to their life, but crowded a lifetime into a few years. Now there are those who are trying to have transplants in order to live to be one hundred, and vegetate.

Well, that's not what we are here for. We're here to fulfill scripture, and no matter what appears on the outside I promise you: you will not die. You cannot go to eternal death in that which cannot die. You are the God of the living, not the dead - dreaming of death, of birth, health and illness, poverty and wealth. You have never left your eternal home. Your descent was in consciousness and it is in consciousness that you will ascend.

Now let us go into the silence.

Also Available from This Author

TITLE	ISBN
Walk by Faith	9781603867474
Imagination Creates Reality	9781603867467
Come, O Blessed & Other Sermons	9781603867450
Behold the Dreamer Cometh and Other Sermons	9781603867443
An Assured Understanding & Other Sermons	9781603867436
A Divine Event and Other Essays	9781603867429
All Things Are Possible	9781603867405
Neville Goddard: The Essential Collection	9781603866781
At Your Command	9781603866774
You Can Never Outgrow I Am	9781603866767
The Secret of Imagining	9781603866750
Neville Goddard: The Complete Reader - Vol 1	9781603866743
Out of This World: Thinking Fourth-Dimensionally	9781603865647
Your Faith Is Your Fortune	9781603865593
Feeling is the Secret	9781603865449
Five Lessons	9781603865357
Three Propositions and Eleven Other Essays	9781603865296
The Power of Awareness	9781603865043
Awakened Imagination	9781603865036
Prayer: The Art of Believing	9781603864978
The Fourth Dimension	1603860266

9 781603 867672